For Betsy

Stephen Dunn

7/2/85

ALSO BY
STEPHEN DUNN

BETWEEN ANGELS

W · W · NORTON & COMPANY · NEW YORK · LONDON

BETWEEN ANGELS

POEMS BY STEPHEN DUNN

The text of this book is composed in 10/13 Linotron 202 Weiss,
with display type set in Augustea Inline.
Composition and Manufacturing by
The Maple-Vail Book Manufacturing Group.
Book design by Antonina Krass.

Acknowledgments appear on page 112.

Library of Congress Cataloging-in-Publication Data
Dunn, Stephen, 1939–
    Between angels.
    I. Title.
PS3554.U49B49   1989   811'.54   88-32962
ISBN 0-393-30658-5
W. W. Norton & Company, Inc., 500 Fifth Avenue, New York, N.Y. 10110
W. W. Norton & Company Ltd., 10 Coptic Street, London, WC1A 1PU
3 4 5 6 7 8 9 0

For Lawrence Raab

CONTENTS

1 | L E A V I N G S

2 | V A R I A T I O N S

3 | URGENCIES

ACKNOWLEDGMENTS

My thanks to the John Simon Guggenheim Foundation for a Fellowship that helped in the writing of some of these poems. Thanks too to The N.J. State Council on the Arts for a Distinguished Artist Fellowship, and to Yaddo for two important residencies. I'm grateful to Stockton State College for its continuing support.

I'm especially indebted to Lawrence Raab for his scrupulous attention to these poems, and to Donald Lawder for his, and to my wife Lois for her great good sense as a first reader. Deep thanks, too, to Irene Feuker for the preparation of the manuscript. An appreciative nod to Mary Lisa Walker for the title "Dancing with God."

I

LEAVINGS

THE GUARDIAN ANGEL

Afloat between lives and stale truths,
　　he realizes
he's never truly protected one soul,

they all die anyway, and what good
　　is solace,
solace is cheap. The signs are clear:

the drooping wings, the shameless thinking
　　about utility
and self. It's time to stop.

The guardian angel lives for a month
　　with other angels,
sings the angelic songs, is reminded

that he doesn't have a human choice.
　　The angel of love
lies down with him, and loving

restores to him his pure heart.
　　Yet how hard it is
to descend into sadness once more.

When the poor are evicted, he stands
　　between them
and the bank, but the bank sees nothing

in its way. When the meek are overpowered
    he's there, the thin air
through which they fall. Without effect

he keeps getting in the way of insults.
    He keeps wrapping
his wings around those in the cold.

Even his lamentations are unheard,
    though now,
in for the long haul, trying to live

beyond despair, he believes, he needs
    to believe
everything he does takes root, hums

beneath the surfaces of the world.

LEAVING THE POLITE PARTY

This time the leaving felt especially good
    as if I'd moved
toward some clean elemental selfishness

only the right people could respect.
    Above me, though,
no visible moon, no trace of those few stars

I could think of as personal
    when I felt lost.
Lost. There's a melodramatist

in every serious man. I merely hadn't found
    enough hearts
in conflict with themselves, enough trouble,

enough joy. Ah, the bucket seat held me
    as if I belonged.
Soon the road was all fast food

and car dealerships, closed, but lit up
    like some mock end
of the world. It was my way home

yet I felt removed, alert, outside
    myself
watching a man drive home

in the sudden strangeness of America,
    past the arches
and signs that guaranteed everything

marked down. On the tape
    Janis Ian lamented
the good old days gone by,

but I wasn't thinking now of loss.
    I saw a billboard
and translated all the words.

How clear everything was! We eat
    and get hungry.
We imagine going wild, but instead

we spend. Texaco was on my left,
    Prudential up ahead,
and I recognized without anticipation

these were the landmarks I'd so often
    told others they'd see
before it was necessary to turn.

BEYOND HAMMONTON

Night is longing, longing, longing,
beyond all endurance.
                              —Henry Miller

The back roads I've traveled late
at night, alone, a little drunk,
wishing I were someone
on whom nothing is lost,

are the roads by day I take
to the car wash in Hammonton
or to Blue Anchor's
lawnmower repair shop
when the self-propel mechanism goes.

Fascinating how the lamplight
that's beckoned
from solitary windows
gives way to white shutters
and occasionally a woman
in her yard, bending over
something conspicuously in bloom.

So much then is duty, duty, duty,
and so much
with the sun visor tilted
and destination known
can be endured.

But at night . . . no, even at night
so much can be endured.

I've known only one man
who left the road,
followed an intriguing light
to its source.
He told me
that he knocked many times
before it became clear to him
he must break down the door.

KINDNESS

In Manhattan, I learned a public kindness
    was a triumph
over the push of money, the constrictions

of fear. If it occurred it came
    from some deep
primal memory, almost entirely lost—

Here, let me help you, then you me,
    otherwise we'll die.
Which is why I love the weather

in Minnesota, every winter kindness
    linked
to obvious self-interest,

thus so many kindnesses
    when you need them;
praise blizzards, praise the cold.

Kindness of any kind shames me,
    makes me remember
what I haven't done or been.

I met a woman this summer in Aspen
    so kind
I kept testing her to see

where it would end. I thought: how easy
    to be kind in Aspen,
no poverty or crime, each day

a cruise in the blond, expensive streets.
    But I was proof
it wasn't easy, there was an end

to her kindness and I found it;
    I kept wanting
what she didn't have

until she gave me what I deserved.
    If the hearts of men
are merciless, as James Wright said,

then any kindness is water turned
    to wine, it's manna
in the new and populous desert.

The stranger in me knows
    what strangers need.
It might be better to turn us away.

MEN TALK

It was the winter I had to get away.
Though I didn't know it then,
I needed the kind of solace
you get at depressing movies
if they're good; all those others
just like you. In Orlando,
biding time, I watched peacocks
among people in a wooded preserve,
then drove further inland past cattle
to where my friend lived.

I was glad the peacocks made awful
sounds, and I was glad—
after we jogged his circular path
through the orange groves—
that our polite, complete sentences
broke down into talk
of his empty house, the woman who left,
and then my house far away.
I told him what staying meant, as if
I knew; the precipice in every room.
Friendship: someone leaning
to your side of the truth.

Next day was beautiful,
seventy-five degrees, and each of us
silent, back in control.
We walked into the countryside,
pointed away from ourselves
toward the landscape,

took possession of it for a while.
Kumquats were growing next to lemons
and white birds rode the backs of cows.
Though it wasn't, it seemed enough,
seemed we'd never have to speak again.

FLAWS

I had been worrying once again
   about sad lives
and almost perfect art, Van Gogh,

Kafka, so when that voice on the radio
   sang about drinking
a toast to those who most survive

the lives they've led, I drank that toast
   in the prayerless
sanctum of my room, I said it

out loud in a hush. Then I thought
   of Dr. Williams
who toward the end apologized

to his wife for doing everything
   he had loved to do.
He was speaking of course to death,

not to her, though death instructed him
   how valuable she was.
I thought of a lamp the neighbor's child

had broken, then pieced back together
   with wires and glue.
And my friend, the good husband,

kissing the scars his wife brought home
    after the mastectomy.
I drank that toast again, though silently.

The radio was playing something old
    and bad
I once thought was good.

Flaws. Suddenly the act of trying
    to say how it feels
to live a life, to say it flawlessly,

seemed more immense than ever. Then
    I remembered
those Persian rug makers built them in,

the flaws, because only Allah was perfect.
    What arrogance to think
that otherwise they wouldn't be there!

I allowed myself to wonder
    about the ethics
of repair, but just for a while.

Sleep, too, was on my mind
    and I knew
the difficulty that lay ahead:

how hard I'd try when I couldn't,
    how it would come
if only I could find a way

to enter and drift without concern
    for what it is.

COMPANIONSHIP

The last time I climbed a mountain
my friend from the West
called it a hill, but it was
a mountain to me,
a few thousand feet, Vermont,
my feet hurting
almost all the way.
Never again, I swore,
would I go against my body
for the sake of companionship,
though maybe I just
should have sworn off mountains,
the tops of them in particular,
those invitations
made to us since childhood,
so hard to refuse.
My friend, a Brooklyn boy,
lived in Colorado and had learned
that something like God
lived there too.
I was to climb, he said,
without desire,
one step and then the next.
I was to love the sides
as much as the top,
the wildflowers along the way,
the rocks.
I desired the top to come
down to me. Mid-way
I desired the little parking lot

at the base where my Subaru
waited with its cushions and wings.
At the top, we shook hands
but did not hug. What we'd done
was too small for that,
and there still was the getting down,
a few different ways
I could disappoint him,
as any unequal partner knows,
just by being who I was.

LOVELINESS

Years ago, when I was rotten with virtue,
  I believed loveliness
was just a face, a flower,

no underside to it, no dark complication.
  Sometime later
I was sure it couldn't be more than this:

a group of us singing "We Shall Overcome,"
  hands joined, 1968,
the double elixir of anger and conviction

making us gravely intimate.
  But I've felt
the loveliness of a fine moment

passing into the moment that follows,
  I've read books
that slowed down a life

long enough for me to enter it, a life
  so dangerous
and short I've started to rage

at all the postponements in mine,
  all the dead
unforgivably correct afternoons . . .

Last year in a room where survivors
　　were gathered
I watched one man's obstinate calm

when it was his turn to thank God,
　　how he kept what was his
his, the lovely discrepancy

between what the world expected
　　and what he gave.
Or perhaps he was just shy, and I made him

into a man I needed just then. Either way
　　I was happy
to witness and be part of something

that ever-so-little could rock the heart,
　　tip it
toward fullness. Tonight the anchorman

offers up the brutal in an even voice,
　　and the camera zooms in
to the strange loveliness of a bruise;

it reminds me of what a child wrote
　　about a sad flower:
the yellow thing in the middle was blue.

EMPTINESS

I've heard yogis talk of a divine
    emptiness,
the body free of its base desires,

some coiled and luminous god
    in all of us
waiting to be discovered . . .

        and always I've pivoted,

followed Blake's road of excess
    to the same source
and know how it feels to achieve

nothing, the nothing that exists
    after accomplishment.
And I've known the emptiness

of nothing to say, no reason to move,
    those mornings I've built
a little cocoon with the bedcovers

and lived in it, almost happily,
    because what fools
the body more than warmth?

        And more than once

I've shared an emptiness with someone
     and learned
how generous I can be—here,

take this, take this . . .

WAITING

Moments ago something cruel—
   one of those empty trains
      they send by,

some phantom express—caught me
   leaning, readying myself.
      Now the man next to me

turns up the sound, a big silver radio
   on his shoulder,
      his eyes closed.

He wants it loud and bad
   to obliterate some anxiety
      of his own.

What to do but lecture him
   on public versus private,
      or smash his radio

into little bits of quiet?
   But I move away instead,
      look down that long stretch

of track for what is overdue,
   maybe powerless somewhere
      like a messiah.

It's a clear blue day, not a limit
   in sight.
      I'm late for love

and love is famous for not waiting well,
   for conjuring its enemies
      after minutes.

The man with radio dons earphones,
   starts to move,
      a dancer so solo

there's no chance he could be reached,
   ever. Suddenly
      a thousand low voices

seem to be saying my name—
   the train coming in
      like something once desired,

now too late to save the day
   . . . and no one visible
      to blame.

ON THE WAY TO WORK

Life is a bitch. And then you die.
                    —a bumper sticker

I hated bumper stickers, hated
the notion of wanting to be known
by one glib or earnest thing.
But this time I sped up to see
a woman in her forties, cigarette,
no way to tell how serious
she was, to what degree she felt
the joke, or what she wanted from us
who'd see it, philosophers all.
If I'd had my own public answer—
"New Hope For The Dead,"
the only sticker I almost stuck—
I would have driven in front of her
and slowed down. How could we not
have become friends
or the kind of enemies
who must talk into the night,
just one mistake away from love?
I rode parallel to her,
glancing over, as one does
on an airplane at someone's book.
Short, straight hair. No make-up.
A face that had been a few places
and only come back from some.
At the stop light I smiled
at her, then made my turn
toward the half-life of work
past the placebo shops
and the beautiful park, white

like a smokescreen with snow.
She didn't follow, not in this
bitch of a life.
And I had so much to tell her
before we die
about what I'd done all these years
in between, under, and around
truths like hers. Who knows
where we would have stopped?

ALMOST HOME

Moonlight in the poplars,
moonlight all the way down
to my shoes

and, in memory, the dog bark
of a fox
before the rabbit squealed.

Just a hundred yards or so
to home, this
the back and quickest way

from my neighbor's house.
The night birds aren't singing
of rue and woe;

that's just me, listening.
These are my woods,
if woods are anyone's.

No, these woods
are unkeepable. Tonight
I can feel every small thing

looking for a smaller thing.
That's what delicious is.
That's fear.

The owl must descend
and the mouse be lifted
into another world.

Blind is what I need to be,
says the mole.
I don't even have a prayer.

PRIVILEGE

. . . the privilege of ordinary heartbreak.
—Nadezhda Mandelstam

I have had such privilege
    and have wept
the admittedly small tears

that issue from it, and for years
    have expected
some terrible random tax

for being born or staying alive.
    It has not come,
though recently in the neighborhood

a child's red ball got loose
    from her, with traffic
bearing down. She was not my child,

I was so happy she was not
    my child.
If one could choose, who wouldn't

settle for deceit or betrayal,
    something
that could be argued or forgiven?

And when I think of Osip, his five
    thousand miles
on a prison train, and the package

you sent him returned months later,
     "The addressee is dead,"
well, that's when the mind that hunts

for comparisons should hesitate,
     then seek
its proper silence. History pressed in

and down, Nadezhda, and you kept living
     and found the words.
I intend no comparison when I say

today the odor of lilacs outside
     my window
is half perfume, half something rotten.

That's just how they smell
     and what I'm used to,
one thing and always the disturbing

insistence of another, fat life itself,
     too much
to let in, too much to turn away.

TENDERNESS

Back then when so much was clear
    and I hadn't learned
young men learn from women

what it feels like to feel just right,
    I was twenty-three,
she thirty-four, two children, a husband

in prison for breaking someone's head.
    Yelled at, slapped
around, all she knew of tenderness

was how much she wanted it, and all
    I knew
were back seats and a night or two

in a sleeping bag in the furtive dark.
    We worked
in the same office, banter and loneliness

leading to the shared secret
    that to help
National Biscuit sell biscuits

was wildly comic, which led to my body
    existing with hers
like rain that's found its way underground

to water it naturally joins.
    I can't remember
ever saying the exact word, tenderness,

though she did. It's a word I see now
    you must be older to use,
you must have experienced the absence of it

often enough to know what silk and deep balm
    it is
when at last it comes. I think it was terror

at first that drove me to touch her
    so softly,
then selfishness, the clear benefit

of doing something that would come back
    to me twofold,
and finally, sometime later, it became

reflexive and motiveless in the high
    ignorance of love.
Oh abstractions are just abstract

until they have an ache in them. I met
    a woman never touched
gently, and when it ended between us

I had new hands and new sorrow,
    everything it meant
to be a man changed, unheroic, floating.

SWEETNESS

Just when it has seemed I couldn't bear
    one more friend
waking with a tumor, one more maniac

with a perfect reason, often a sweetness
    has come
and changed nothing in the world

except the way I stumbled through it,
    for a while lost
in the ignorance of loving

someone or something, the world shrunk
    to mouth-size,
hand-size, and never seeming small.

I acknowledge there is no sweetness
    that doesn't leave a stain,
no sweetness that's ever sufficiently sweet . . .

Tonight a friend called to say his lover
    was killed in a car
he was driving. His voice was low

and guttural, he repeated what he needed
    to repeat, and I repeated
the one or two words we have for such grief

until we were speaking only in tones.
    Often a sweetness comes
as if on loan, stays just long enough

to make sense of what it means to be alive,
    then returns to its dark
source. As for me, I don't care

where it's been, or what bitter road
    it's traveled
to come so far, to taste so good.

BETWEEN ANGELS

Between angels, on this earth
absurdly between angels, I
try to navigate

in the bluesy middle ground
of desire and withdrawal,
in the industrial air,
among the bittersweet

efforts of people to connect,
make sense, endure.
The angels out there,
what are they?

Old helpers, half-believed,
or dazzling better selves,
imagined,

that I turn away from
as if I preferred
all the ordinary, dispiriting
tasks at hand?

I shop in the cold
neon aisles
thinking of pleasure,
I kiss my paycheck

a mournful kiss goodbye
thinking of pleasure,
in the evening replenish

my drink, make a choice
to read or love or watch,
and increasingly I watch.
I do not mind living

like this. I cannot bear
living like this.
Oh, everything's true
at different times

in the capacious day,
just as I don't forget
and always forget

half the people in the world
are dispossessed.
Here chestnut oaks
and tenements

make their unequal claims.
Someone thinks of betrayal.
A child spills her milk;
I'm on my knees cleaning it up—

sponge, squeeze, I change nothing,
just move it around.
The inconsequential floor
is beginning to shine.

II

VARIATIONS

BEGINNINGS

Never the natural world
except when its beauty
is arguable, perverse,
but always the abundance
of what it means
to be a person, alone
and with others,
this is what makes me
want to gather myself
as conjurer and witness,
and why, for example,
in this photograph
of my parents at a resort
before I was born,
the bougainvillea behind them
is only spectacular,
while they seem to contain
some mysterious explanation,
not just to my birth,
but to the development
of lives in general.
Such stopped happiness here!
So tempting to imagine them
as I need to, the son,
the revisionist.
He's leaning her way,
his white suit cleanly pressed,
and she's in white too, lacy
all the way to her ankles.
They're any couple in love,

strange and ordinary
as seeds that turn
into forsythia or grass.
How unfair it would be
to speak to them of history
or the likely drift of things.
It's Havana, mid-July,
they walk back to their room
where a fan is slowly turning
The burden of their clothing
disappears. There's a slash
of afternoon sun on the carpet,
which they don't see,
nor do they know
the chambermaid, on her way
to turn down the covers
and leave a mint, has smiled
at the sign on the door.
Miles away, sugar cane
is growing in orderly rows,
but in that room
beyond the photograph
only the wild, slippery present
exists, a beginning
among beginnings,
the child all grown up
now choosing the angle of entry,
the love cries, the aftermath.

EACH FROM DIFFERENT HEIGHTS

That time I thought I was in love
and calmly said so
was not much different from the time
I was truly in love
and slept poorly and spoke out loud
to the wall
and discovered the hidden genius
of my hands.
And the times I felt less in love,
less than someone,
were, to be honest, not so different
either.
Each was ridiculous in its own way
and each was tender, yes,
sometimes even the false is tender.
I am astounded
by the various kisses we're capable of.
Each from different heights
diminished, which is simply the law.
And the big bruise
from the longer fall looked perfectly white
in a few years.
That astounded me most of all.

THE STORYTELLER

God was listening, but even so
    I never told the truth
in confession. If I'd stolen candy

from Woolworths, I'd say I took
    the Lord's name
in vain eleven times, Father,

since my last confession. If I'd
    been good,
I'd say I took the Lord's name

six or seven times. I knew the priest
    depended on sins
to feel good about his job,

but most of all I wanted to get back
    to the religion
of the schoolyard as fast as possible,

to epiphanous spin moves off the post
    and soft reverse layups.
Thus I never properly did penance

at the altar, two Hail Mary's
    instead of four,
a fast Our Father, maybe half

an Act of Contrition or Apostles'
   Creed.
I don't know why I never was afraid

of God and his famous penchant
   for punishment.
I don't know why Hell

didn't scare me, why it seemed
   like some movie
with special effects. Angels, though,

were real, like invisible friends
   you could count on.
I remember thinking angels could make

a shot go in, angels were what prayers
   were all about.
When my friend Brian said

he was going to confess to Father Kelly
   that he masturbated,
I told him look, no, don't stir up

Father Kelly, tell him you took
   the Lord's name in vain
three hundred times and were very sorry,

but Brian said God was listening,
   God *knew*,
and anyway he would be forgiven,

that was the thing about being Catholic,
    stupid, your sins
could be forgiven. I knew he was right,

but I went right on confessing
    to Jesus Christs,
goddamns, Christs Almighty, words

I never in fact said, but words I knew
    were the right words
for the occasion.

THE SACRED

After the teacher asked if anyone had
     a sacred place
and the students fidgeted and shrank

in their chairs, the most serious of them all
     said it was his car,
being in it alone, his tape deck playing

things he'd chosen, and others knew the truth
     had been spoken
and began speaking about their rooms,

their hiding places, but the car kept coming up,
     the car in motion,
music filling it, and sometimes one other person

who understood the bright altar of the dashboard
     and how far away
a car could take him from the need

to speak, or to answer, the key
     in having a key
and putting it in, and going.

DANCING WITH GOD

At first the surprise
of being singled out,
the dance floor crowded
and me not looking my best,
a too-often-worn dress
and the man with me
a budding casualty
of one repetition too much.
God just touched his shoulder
and he left.
Then the confirmation of
an old guess:
God was a wild god,
into the most mindless rock,
but graceful,
looking—this excited me—
like no one I could love,
cruel mouth, eyes evocative
of promises unkept.
I never danced better, freer,
as if dancing were my way
of saying how easily
I could be with him, or apart.
When the music turned slow
God held me close
and I felt for a moment
I'd mistaken him,
that he was Death
and this the famous embrace
before the lights go out.

But God kept holding me
and I him
until the band stopped
and I stood looking at a figure
I wanted to slap
or forgive for something,
I couldn't decide which.
He left then, no thanks,
no sign
that he'd felt anything
more than an earthly moment
with someone who could've been
anyone on earth.
To this day I don't know why
I thought he was God,
though it was clear
there was no going back
to the man who brought me,
nice man
with whom I'd slept
and grown tired,
who danced wrong,
who never again
could do anything right.

THE LISTENER

The town was nameless because it could
    have been any town
one was new to, alone in, and he walked

its main street with a hesitant sense
    of possibility,
a sizing up, all the shops in a row,

this open door or that. He stopped
    to look in a window,
and, seeing no one but himself in the glass,

corrected a few strands of hair.
    In the street
women were everywhere, prolific

because he chose to see them
    singularly.
He was after all a traveler, alert

to the small deprivations that travelers—
    suspended as they are—
notice and feel. The women in the town

were secretly waiting to be spoken to,
    deeply,
some unaddressed part of them

closed down for too long. And he knew
    the words, interrogative,
concerned, and how to wait for an answer,

showing with his eyes how much he wanted it
    until it came.
Most of them had never known such intimacy,

a man listening, the extraordinary fact
    of a man listening,
which was like a touch to them,

a touch, say, on the forehead
    when they felt
totally exposed. He entered

The Half Moon Cafe. A man
    with a John Deere hat
sat alone. Two women, lonely, he knew,

because of their public voices,
    were finishing dessert.
It always went like this. He'd ask

something about the town. Then he'd ask
    something else.

THE KISSER AND TELLER

He didn't know the stories
we tell about them
are always about us,

and how could he?
Listening to other men
over the years

he'd only heard
the men they wanted to be
and the men they became

one story at a time.
Their buddies would click
glasses, smile, the familiar

litany—stacked, nympho,
piece—making all of them
dreamy and close.

Everything he desired,
everything good he felt
got mixed up

with a literature
he didn't know he knew:
Madonnas, Circes, lovely ladies

without mercy.
A part of him would disappear
if he dared to love them,

wasn't that written somewhere?
Thus his primal strut
afterwards, all the details . . .

THE MAN WHO CLOSED SHOP

To allow himself to be properly held
   he had to let his body
soften, give it unguarded, willingly,

to her. It meant suspension
   of achievement,
a celebration in a country

without government. Always he desired
   the getting there,
loved, in fact, getting lost

on the way. But too often,
   too soon,
he'd think of the office

or a program he was missing
   on T.V.   He'd feel
his body pull back into itself

like a man closing his own shop
   mid-day
for reasons he didn't understand.

He'd roll away, thinking to himself
   "This is pleasure, too,"
knowing he'd need different words—

yet whatever his explanation
   she knew it
beforehand, several touches ago.

MON SEMBLABLE

No man has ever dared to describe
himself as he truly is.

—Camus

I like things my way
every chance I get.
A limit doesn't exist

when it comes to that.
But please, don't confuse
what I say with honesty.

Isn't honesty the open yawn
the unimaginative love
more than truth?

Anonymous among strangers
I look for those
with hidden wings,

and for scars
that those who once had wings
can't hide.

Though I know it's unfair,
I reveal myself
one mask at a time.

Does this appeal to you,
such slow disclosures,
a lifetime perhaps

of almost knowing one another?
I would hope you, too,
would hold something back,

and that you'd always want
whatever unequal share
you had style enough to get.

Altruism is for those
who can't endure their desires.
There's a world

as ambiguous as a moan,
a pleasure moan
our earnest neighbors

might think a crime.
It's where we could live.
I'll say I love you,

which will lead, of course,
to disappointment,
but those words unsaid

poison every next moment.
I will try to disappoint you
better than anyone ever has.

LETTING THE PUMA GO

*I'll make a perfect body, said God,
and invent ways to make it fail.*
      —lines removed from the poem

He liked to watch the big cats.
He liked their beautiful contempt,
yet imagined how they might change
and love him
and stretch out near his feet
if he were to let them go.
And of course he wanted
to let them go
as he wanted to let himself go,
grateful for the iron bars, the lock.
He'd heard the tiger succeeds
only once in twenty hunts—
the fragile are that attuned
and that fast—
and was confused again about God,
the god who presided here.
He'd watch the tigers at feeding time,
then turn to the black panther,
its languid fierce pacing, and know
it was possible not to care
if the handsome get everything.
Except for the lions.
Hadn't the lions over the years
become their names, like the famous?
But he could spend half an afternoon
with those outfielders,
the pumas, cheetahs, leopards.
So this is excellence, he imagined:
movement toward the barely possible,

the puma's dream
of running down a hummingbird
on a grassy plain.
And then he'd let the puma go;
just before closing time
he'd wish-open its cage
and follow it into the suddenly
uncalm streets,
telling all the children it was his.

HIS MUSIC

It wasn't that he liked being miserable.
He simply had grown used to wearing
a certain face, become comfortable
with his assortment of shrugs and sighs.
His friends said How are you?—
and prepared their sympathy cards.
Miserable was his style, his insurance
against life's frightening, temporary joys.
And when the truly awful happened,
some rejection or loss,
how ready he was for its aftermath,
how appropriate his posture, his words.
Yet when she said she loved him
something silently wild and molecular
began its revolution; he would've smiled
if the news from the distant provinces
of his body had reached him in time.
He frowned. And did not allow the short sigh
which would have meant pleasure
but now, alone, was just old breath
escaping, the long ahhhh, that music
which soothed him, and was his song.

COMPETITION

Because he played games seriously
   and therefore knew grace
comes hard, rises through the cheap

in us, the petty, the entire history
   of our defeats,
he looked for grace in his opponents,

found a few friends that way
   and so many others
he could never drink with, talk to.

He learned early never to let up,
   never to give
a weaker opponent a gift

because so many times he'd been
   that person
and knew the humiliation in it,

being pandered to, a bone for the sad
   dog.
And because he remembered those times

after a loss when he'd failed
   at grace—
stole from the victor

the pleasures of pure victory
   by speaking
about a small injury or the cold

he wasn't quite over—he loved
   those opponents
who'd shake hands and give credit,

save their true and bitter stories
   for their lovers, later,
when all such lamentations are comic,

the sincere *if onlys* of grown men
   in short pants.
Oh there were people who thought

all of it so childish; what to say
   to them, how to agree,
ever, about dignity and fairness?

LUCK

At the blackjack table he felt it
   move
to the dealer, then back to him.

How many times, it threatened,
   can you not act
on what you feel?   But he had a wife

and children and a house with extra
   rooms.
He bet small, and luck wouldn't stay

long enough to make a difference,
   there were others,
always there were others calling it,

asking it to fill the empty spaces,
   postpone the ugly world.
He understood it didn't belong

to him, and how dangerous it was
   to love it more
than it might allow. Too sane! Too sane!

cried luck from across the room,
   and came back
to his table just to be bad.

WITHDRAWAL

The landscape had had its moments
    but now was verdant
and fixed. No longer did he desire
even its pleasing little deaths.
    Emergence,
decay, what else was new?
The birds repeated themselves.
    The peonies
like beautiful women
were better if ignored.

Now and then a woman would walk
    under the large oaks,
her obvious sadness
making everything else disappear.
    And once
he saw a man dig up
something metal near the roses,
    sunlight
hitting it like a new kind of love.
Then people together on the grass,
    collecting the shadows
from the trees. He liked how they stole
from the landscape, drew the sky down.

Yet up close they had their odors
    and errors
of style, and so many of them
could be heard speaking innocently
    of blossom and flight.

He hated how he resembled them,
these changelings he could see
   were as fixed
as the landscape itself.
And he wanted not to need them
   so much;
if only he could find a way
through the entanglements, perhaps
   to a clearing
beyond the garden and the trees,
if there might be a clearing.

THE MAN WHO WOULD BE THEIRS

He tried to hide
in a hiding place so white
he'd be found
and wondered about.
He wore black.
It seemed just a matter of time.
No one, though, saw his tracks,
clear as they were.
No one seemed to know
he was gone.
And it got cold
on the mountain,
in that snow.
What was he to do,
find himself a regular job?
No, he came back
to say where he was hiding.
He owed them that, he felt,
then showed them
how they might get lost
unless they listened carefully,
unless of course
they wished to get lost,
in which case
he was the wrong man
for them to find.
It's been months now.
He builds fires, waits.

He can see all the way down
to the village.
It's still his village,
he thinks,
even if, and no matter what.

WANTING TO GET CLOSER

Oh vanity
makes everything a little lovelier.
I like those people
who feel a vagueness exists
without them, who see in themselves
a hundred possible improvements.
And the fictions! How the thing
looked at changes as it changes
the looker. Even the physicist
stands here rather than there
tipping the universe accordingly.

To speak of Narcissus is to speak
of conviction. What matter
that he saw himself
in the glassy water?   For once
his aesthetic found its embodiment
and he went to meet it, dying
(I'd like to think) of amazement.
Reader, whom I must not address,
once again I'm standing
in front of a mirror.
I want to get close, then closer.
The image doesn't interest me.

III

URGENCIES

TO A TERRORIST

For the historical ache, the ache passed down
which finds its circumstance and becomes
the present ache, I offer this poem

without hope, knowing there's nothing,
not even revenge, which alleviates
a life like yours. I offer it as one

might offer his father's ashes
to the wind, a gesture
when there's nothing else to do.

Still, I must say to you:
I hate your good reasons.
I hate the hatefulness that makes you fall

in love with death, your own included.
Perhaps you're hating me now,
I who own my own house

and live in a country so muscular,
so smug, it thinks its terror is meant
only to mean well, and to protect.

Christ turned his singular cheek,
one man's holiness another's absurdity.
Like you, the rest of us obey the sting,

the surge. I'm just speaking out loud
to cancel my silence. Consider it an old impulse,
doomed to become mere words.

The first poet probably spoke to thunder
and, for a while, believed
thunder had an ear and a choice.

CLARITIES

Now dusk mixes with the fog
   like an ambassador come down
     by helicopter
to live without explanation

among the rural poor. The street
   is invisible. It's 4:43,
     January 8,
the year of the digital,

of the too much precision to bear.
   The weatherman said cold air
     coming in
from Pennsylvania. He said sleet

then snow then clearing then—
   speaking to me—days of
     uncertainty.
Once again there seemed room for me

in the world. The streetlamps are chalky,
   blurred. I've turned
     to them,
having just read how a young girl

was tortured to death in Chile,
   her father forced
     to watch.
Sometimes solace won't do,

and there's no sleeping with what
   you know, and advice
      is obscene.
Sometimes there's a pity

only the self can give, amniotic,
   a total curling in.
      I wish
they had killed him, the father,

allowed some end to what he saw.
   So much that is human
      was alien by then.
I must stop thinking of myself.

It's 5:22. I have to be somewhere soon.
   I have to walk out
      into the fog
and take my place among the blind.

The torturers go with me now, calm,
   exact. They want nothing
      withheld. And
everything the bastards do is in the name

of necessity and in the name of the good.

FORGIVENESS

The torturer removes a fingernail:
   No forgiveness for him.
An old Nazi softens, laments:
   No, put him to death.
He who hates:
   Give him a mirror and a gun.
He who hates in the singular:
   Forgive him, once.
The crimes of lovers:
   Forgive them later, as soon as you can.
Anyone who hurts someone you love:
   Saints, you forgivers,
                we could never be friends.
The betrayer, the liar, the thief:
   Forgive anything you might do yourself.
The terrorist pulls a pin:
   Forgive the desperate, the homeless,
            the crazed.
The terrorist pulls a pin:
   No, no more good reasons.
The rat in my crawlspace, the vicious rat:
   No forgiveness necessary.
I, who put out the poison:
   God of rats, forgive me once again.

HAWK

What a needy, desperate thing
to claim what's wild for oneself,
yet the hawk circling above the pines
looks like the same one I thought

might become mine after it crashed
into the large window and lay
one wing spread, the other loosely
tucked, then no, not dead, got up

dazed, and in minutes was gone.
Now once again
this is its sky, this its woods.
The tasty small birds it loves

have seen their God and know
the suddenness of such love
as we know lightning or flash flood.
If hawks can learn, this hawk learned

what's clear can be hard
down where the humans live,
and that the hunting isn't good
where the air is such a lie.

It glides above the pines and I
turn back into the room, the hawk book
open on the cluttered table
to Cooper's Hawk

and the unwritten caption:
that to be wild
means nothing you do or have done
needs to be explained.

ABOUT THE ELK AND THE
COYOTES THAT KILLED HER CALF

FOR RICHARD SELZER

The coyotes know it's just
    a matter of time,
but the elk will not let them

have her calf. You describe
    how they attack
and pull back, and how she goes on

repelling them, occasionally licking
    her calf's face,
until exhausted she turns

and gives it all up. So the elk,
    with her fierce
and futile resistance in which we

recognize something to admire,
    is held up
against the brilliant, wild

cunning of the coyotes.
    I love your sense
that the natural world stinks

and is beautiful and how important it is
    to have favorites.
Some part of us we'd like to believe

is essentially us, sides with the elk.
   Ah but tomorrow,
desperate, and night falling fast

and with a different sense of family . . .

WHITE FLAMINGOS AT 37,000 FEET

There's talk of foreclosure
in the choiceless wind.
There are men on tractors
trying to do it all themselves
as their fathers did.
And one woman I know, town-bred,
who got into it for love,
still scattering seed
for the chickens.
I remember buying eggs, brown,
with flecks of blood.
I remember the grain silos
like busy cathedrals,
and how everyone
talked weather, which was money.

The man next to me
is reading about flamingos.
Remove pink shrimp, he says,
from their diets, and they lose
color, become white, foolish.
A zoo discovered it: white
flamingos! What's the world
coming to, he wants to know.

The sky is cloudless, clear,
and I've a window seat.
All the children are leaving
for the cities. The conglomerates

are making chickens
more efficient. And, now,
this pale knowledge.
That old crazy quilt of squares
and rectangles is beautiful today,
seemingly commodious,
so many little moving things
down there.

CLEANLINESS

My cat in a patch of sun
    on the floor, my cat
to whom everything is natural,

puts a little spit on her paws
    and touches herself clean.
Pussy: an epithet, insulting.

Or redeemed, a lover's word
    when only the vulgar
is equal to our wild good humor.

My pussycat in a patch of sun
    licking away
all that's accumulated . . .

Cleanliness; if only we believed,
    without guilt,
in the tongue's intelligence

and the wisdom of genitals,
    wouldn't that erase
a few dirty words?   He sucks,

for example. She sucks. How lovely
    as words of praise.
Now my cat, spit-clean,

in a crouch, tail going,
    she's seen
something she wants

and what lover of cats
    wouldn't admire
how perfectly she's made for this?

HAPPINESS

A state you must dare not enter
    with hopes of staying,
quicksand in the marshes, and all

the roads leading to a castle
    that doesn't exist.
But there it is, as promised,

with its perfect bridge above
    the crocodiles,
and its doors forever open.

URGENCIES

I woke to the sound of rain, and lay there
   canceling
parts of the day. Now I couldn't patch

the leaking roof; something funny
   about that,
one of the temporary pleasures

of the mind. My wife was still asleep.
   I wanted to disturb her,
tell her about the irony of rain

and Saturday mornings and leaks.
   I put on my robe,
went to the window. In the grayness

there were different shades of gray.
   I don't know why
that seemed sad, or why

I suddenly wanted to pull apart
   the curtains,
let some cruelty in. The rain

was steady and this was spring.
   There were things
to be happy for, the flowers for example,

the tree frogs and their alto songs.
   I wanted to tell my wife
about the grass as if she'd never

heard of grass, the crazy speed at which
   it grows in May,
a few things I'd thought of and noticed

since the night had passed. But her sleep
   was persistent,
a deep and now annoying sleep.

I went downstairs. The cat was waiting
   to be fed and had practiced
certain gestures of affection,

which I loved, so I'd open the can.
   It was understood;
if he'd purr and rub his head

against mine, all anxiety would end,
   the morning
become languorous and his.

I put the coffee on and broke the eggs.
   It was the wooden spoon,
the flame and me against the protoplasmic

sprawl; we made the center hold.
   I wanted my wife
down here, I wanted her in some usual

place doing some usual things.
　　What I had to say to her
was so insignificant only she would understand.

I sat down to eat. The rain picked up.
　　A man could die
just like that. Or begin to slide.

I started to clank the dishes,
　　make some noise.

FATHER, MOTHER, ROBERT HENLEY WHO HANGED HIMSELF IN THE NINTH GRADE, ET AL.

I've sensed ghosts more than once,
    their presence
a kind of plucking from the memorious air.

Always they reveal themselves as lost,
    surviving
on what's loose in me, some last words

I never said, some I did. I've heard
    they can't live
if fully embraced, if taken fully in,

yet I do nothing but listen to their
    wingless hovering,
the everything they never say.

If only I could give them what they need,
    no, if only
I could convince myself these things

must die as naturally as apples
    on the apple tree . . .
but that's in Nature, which is never

wrong, just thoughtless and without shame.

A KIND OF BLINDNESS
AND A KIND OF WARMTH

After the tennis match when my heart
     wouldn't stop its extra
movement, and the tingling in my left hand

brought back my father's last afternoon,
     my mother's
great gasp and eventual silence,

I had things to say I couldn't seem to say
     in daylight.
I needed a dark room, a glass of scotch,

or my head between my wife's breasts,
     a kind of blindness
and a kind of warmth. I didn't say much,

just some things about my heart
     I'd never said
to her or anyone. Soon it slowed

to normal, the tingling stopped,
     the doctor praised
every little working of my body

but couldn't explain what happened.
     Three years have passed
and I know nothing more about how words

get tremulous, or what it takes to say them.
    I just want to get back
whenever I can to that place

where such speech finds permission,
    though often it's not speech
I'm after, my childish mouth opening

a little, then closing, the silence too
    that flowers there.

COLLECTING FUTURE LIVES

Now that everybody was dead
only he and his brother knew
the blood secrets, the unequal
history each nervous system
keeps and rehearses
into a story, a life.
Over the years they'd agreed
to invent and remember
a long hum of good times,
love breaking through
during card games,
their father teaching them
to skip stones
under the Whitestone Bridge.
The smart liar in them
knew these stories
were for their children
who, that very moment
over dinner, were collecting
their future lives.
But sometimes
in their twice-a-year visits
late at night
when their wives had tired
of the old repetitions,
they'd bring up the silences
in the living room
after a voice had been raised,
father's drinking, mother's
long martyrdom before the gods

of propriety and common sense.
In their mannerisms
each could see the same ghosts.
And if they allowed themselves
to keep talking,
if they'd had enough to drink,
love would be all
that mattered, the love
they were cheated of
and the love they got,
the parental love
that if remembered at all
had been given, they decided,
and therefore could be given again.

THE SOUL BOAT

It was a delicate fifteen inches long,
   gondola shaped,
      but like a gondola
that transported no one who could be seen.

Here, the artist said, I've made this
   soul boat for you,
      hang it from your ceiling
by these six thin strings. And so

my soul boat hangs, as if suspended,
   by its almost
      invisible strings,
and I walk under it wondering

about its necessary cargo and if
   in some way
      the house has changed.
Yesterday the morning turned wrong

with noise: my neighbor cutting down
   all his twenty trees
      to make more lawn.
Chestnut oaks and large black pines.

The vibrations from his saw made the soul
   boat sway;
      one of the strings
came loose, the prow tilted toward the floor.

I was full of rage, but didn't go outside.
  I climbed
     the stepladder to right
the little boat, and I took my time.

SADNESS

It was everywhere, in the streets and houses,
    on farms and now in the air itself.
It had come from history and we were history
    so it had come from us.
I told my artist friends who courted it
    not to suffer
on purpose, not to fall in love
    with sadness
because it would be naturally theirs
    without assistance.
I had sad stories of my own,
    but they made me quiet
the way my parents' failures once did,
    nobody's business
but our own, and, besides, what was left to say
    these days
when the unspeakable was out there being spoken,
    exhausting all sympathy?
Yet, feeling it, how difficult to keep
    the face's curtains
closed—she left, he left, they died—
    the heart rising
into the mouth and eyes, everything so basic,
    so unhistorical
at such times. And then, too, the woes
    of others would get in,
but mostly I was inured and out
    to make a decent buck
or in pursuit of some slippery pleasure

that was sadness disguised.
I found it, it found me, oh
    my artist friends
give it up, just mix your paints,
    stroke,
the strokes unmistakably will be yours.

LONELINESS

So many different kinds,
yet only one vague word.
And the Eskimos
with twenty-six words for snow,

such a fine alertness
to what variously presses down.
Yesterday I saw lovers
hugging in the street,

making everyone around them
feel lonely, and the lovers themselves—
wasn't a deferred loneliness
waiting for them?

There must be words

for what our aged mothers, removed
in those unchosen homes, keep inside,
and a separate word for us
who've sent them there, a word

for the secret loneliness of salesmen,
for how I feel touching you
when I'm out of touch.
The contorted, pocked, terribly ugly man

shopping in the 24-hour supermarket
at 3 a.m.—a word for him—
and something, please,
for this nameless ache here

in this nameless spot.
If we paid half as much attention
to our lives as Eskimos to snow . . .
Still, the little lies,

the never enough.
No doubt there must be Eskimos
in their white sanctums, thinking
just let it fall, accumulate.

NATURALLY

When I die there'll be evidence
   such as this
of a life, everything, all of it,

arranged for effect, and only true
   if believed
to be true, and no matter how sad

a few people might feel,
   I know joy
will be holding out

in some muscled corner
   of their hearts,
the sky will simply darken

at the proper time while the light
   will be blinding
elsewhere, in another language.

THE RETARDED ANGEL

AFTER GEORGE DENNISON

Wordless with a message,
you sit on our shoulders
off-balance, one wing

apparently useless,
haunting us
like a father

who won't judge
his son's sullen
deliberate wish

to be judged.
Other angels have urged us
to change our lives,

but you seem to know
we drift, stumbling
toward even the smallest

improvement. To see you
is to imagine how long
and with what difficulty

it took you to reach us,
years perhaps
of landing elsewhere.

Whoever sent you
must have been desperate
and accidentally brilliant, you

with whom we'd never argue,
the damaged, unnerving,
barely hopeful, last resort.

WALKING THE MARSHLAND

Brigantine Wildlife Refuge, 1987

It was no place for the faithless,
     so I felt a little odd
walking the marshland with my daughters,

Canada geese all around and the blue
     herons just standing there,
safe, and the abundance of swans.

The girls liked saying the words,
     gosling,
egret, whooping crane, and they liked

when I agreed. The casinos were a few miles
     to the east.
I liked saying craps and croupier

and sometimes I wanted to be lost
     in those bright
windowless ruins. It was early April,

the gnats and black flies
     weren't out yet.
The mosquitoes hadn't risen

from their stagnant pools to trouble
     paradise and to give us
the great right to complain.

I loved these girls. The world
   beyond Brigantine
awaited their beauty and beauty

is what others want to own.
   I'd keep that
to myself. The obvious

was so sufficient just then.
   Sandpiper. Red-wing
blackbird. "Yes," I said.

But already we were near the end.
   Praise refuge,
I thought. Praise whatever you can.

Some of these poems have been published or will be published
in the following journals:

The American Poetry Review: "Sadness," "Wanting To Get Closer"

The Denver Quarterly: "Competition," "Withdrawal"

The Georgia Review: "The Kisser & Teller," "Clarities," "Mon Semblable"

Graham House Review: "Privilege," "White Flamingos at 37,000 Feet"

The Iowa Review: "Forgiveness," "The Guardian Angel," "Each from Different Heights"

The Nation: "Collecting Future Lives," "Companionship," "Waiting"

New England Review / Bread Loaf Quarterly: "A Kind of Blindness and a Kind of Warmth,"
    "The Sacred"

The New Yorker: "Between Angels"

Ploughshares: "The Listener"

Poetry: "Loveliness," "Emptiness," "Sweetness," "Tenderness," "On the Way To Work,"
    "His Music" (formerly titled "Portrait"), "The Storyteller (formerly titled "Why I
    Think I'm a Writer"), "Hawk," "Naturally," "Happiness," "Kindness," "Letting the
    Puma Go," "Cleanliness"

Poetry Northwest: "The Soul Boat," "To a Terrorist," "Beyond Hammonton,"
    "Walking the Marshland"

Prairie Schooner: "Almost Home," "Urgencies," "Father, Mother, Robert Henley
    Who Hanged Himself in the Ninth Grade, et al."

Quarterly West: "Beginnings," "Flaws"

Seneca Review: "Men Talk"

Three Rivers Poetry Journal: "About the Elk and the Coyotes that Killed Her Calf"

Triquarterly: "Luck," "The Man Who Closed Shop"

Virginia Quarterly Review: "Dancing with God," "Leaving the Polite Party"

A group of these poems won the Levinson Prize from *Poetry.*

"Tenderness" was chosen to appear in *Pushcart Prize XIII.*